Sewer Inspector

By Geoffrey M. Horn

Reading Consultant: Susan Nations, M.Ed.,
Author/Literacy Coach/Consultant in Literacy Development

Marshall Cavendish
Benchmark
New York

Published by Marshall Cavendish Benchmark
An imprint of Marshall Cavendish Corporation

Other Marshall Cavendish Offices:
Marshall Cavendish International (Asia) Private Limited, 1 New Industrial Road, Singapore 536196 •
Marshall Cavendish International (Thailand) Co Ltd. 253 Asoke, 12th Flr, Sukhumvit 21 Road,
Klongtoey Nua, Wattana, Bangkok 10110, Thailand • Marshall Cavendish (Malaysia) Sdn Bhd,
Times Subang, Lot 46, Subang Hi-Tech Industrial Park, Batu Tiga, 40000 Shah Alam, Selangor
Darul Ehsan, Malaysia

Marshall Cavendish is a trademark of Times Publishing Limited

All websites were available and accurate when this book was sent to press.

Library of Congress Cataloging-in-Publication Data
        Horn, Geoffrey M.
                Sewer inspector / by Geoffrey M. Horn.
        p. cm. — (Dirty and dangerous jobs)
        Includes index.
        ISBN 978-1-60870-178-0
        1. Sewerage—Inspection—Vocational guidance—Juvenile literature.
        2. Sanitary engineers—Juvenile literature. I. Title.
    TD719.H67 2011
    628'.2—dc22   2009049826

Developed for Marshall Cavendish Benchmark by RJF Publishing LLC (www.RJFpublishing.com)
Editor: Amanda Hudson
Design: Westgraphix LLC/Tammy West
Photo Research: Edward A. Thomas
Map Illustrator: Stefan Chabluk
Index: Nila Glikin

Cover: Visitors are led through a storm water sewer in Berlin, Germany.

The photographs in this book are used by permission and through the courtesy of: Cover: AFP/Getty
Images; 4: © Greenshoots Communications/Alamy; 6, 21, 23, 25: AP Images; 8: U.S. Coast Guard photo
by Petty Officer 2nd Class Kyle Niemi; 9: National Geographic/Getty Images; 10: © LENARTOWSKI/
age fotostock; 11: Courtesy Northeast Ohio Regional Sewer District; 12, 16, 28: iStockphoto; 14:
Don Hogan Charles/The New York Times/Redux; 15: GEORGE RIZER/Boston Globe /Landov; 17:
© doug steley/Alamy; 19: DOMINIC LIPINSK/PA Photos/Landov; 26: © Pat Canova/Alamy; 29:
LUKE MACGREGOR/Reuters/Landov.

Printed in Malaysia (T).
135642

CONTENTS

Words defined in the glossary are in **bold** type
the first time they appear in the text.

Going with the Flow

Sewer inspectors must be prepared to spend time below ground in dark, cramped spaces.

Sewers are cramped, dark, and dirty. They carry human waste, foul-smelling gases, and dangerous chemicals. Rats, roaches, and germs that cause disease live there. Sewer inspectors must go down into the sewers. Carrying flashlights and wearing protective gear, they must inspect sewer lines for cracks, leaks, breaks, and clogs. When a problem is found, the inspector must file a work request. Then the inspector may return to the problem area to help the work crew and make sure the repair is done properly.

Why Take the Job?

Inspecting and repairing sewers can be a gritty, grimy, and dangerous job. So why would anyone want to do it? One reason is that inspectors do valuable work. By making sure that waste flows properly through sewer pipes, they help stop pollution. They keep cities and towns clean, healthy, and safe. The work also does not require an advanced degree. For most jobs, inspectors need only a high school diploma. They get on-the-job training. Workers can make good salaries compared to other jobs that do not require a college degree.

New York's Stinkiest?

Rose George is the author of a recent book about sewers called *The Big Necessity*. While doing research for the book, she asked this question: In New York City, the police are known as New York's finest. The firefighters are called New York's bravest. So why is there no nickname for New York's sewer workers, "who keep sewage flowing, and keep disease away"? "We're New York's stinkiest," one sewer inspector joked.

Sewer inspectors help make sure that water flushed from millions of toilets every day does not cause pollution.

It Starts with a Flush

There are more than 350 million toilets in the United States. Each day, huge amounts of waste, water, and toilet paper are flushed away. Toilets are not the only source of **wastewater**. When people shower, brush their teeth, wash their hands, or wash their clothes, wastewater flows down the drain. Factories also create large amounts of wastewater. All this wastewater has to go somewhere.

In the past, untreated wastewater was dumped into U.S. rivers and streams. This caused pollution. Polluted water looks bad, smells bad, tastes bad, and can make people sick. Today, water quality remains a major problem in many parts of the world. Many countries do not have wastewater

Why Do Sewers Smell Bad?

"Sewer gas" is actually a mixture of gases. These gases are released when toilet waste **decays**, or breaks down. One gas is called **hydrogen sulfide**. This gas smells like rotten eggs. Breathing too much hydrogen sulfide can make people very sick. Ammonia is also found in sewer gas. Ammonia can irritate the eyes and nose.

treatment systems. About 40 percent of the world's people do not have access to modern toilets.

The United States has about 1 million miles (1.6 million kilometers) of sewer pipes. If all those pipes were put end to end, they would stretch from the Earth to the Moon and back—twice. The nation's sewer pipes carry wastewater from homes and businesses. This water goes to about 20,000 **sewage treatment plants**. At these plants, the pollution is removed, and the wastewater is made clean and pure enough to drink. Sewer inspectors check all the sewer pipes for problems. They make sure the wastewater is flowing safely and smoothly.

Types of Sewer Systems

Many cities actually have two types of sewer systems. Sewers that carry wastewater are called **sanitary sewers**. ("Sanitary" comes from a Latin word that means "health.") Sewers that handle rain and melting snow are called

How Much Wastewater?

"Each day in the United States, sewer systems carry about 50 trillion gallons (189 trillion liters) of wastewater. At that rate, it would take just three days to fill all of Lake Erie.

storm sewers. In most cases, storm sewers can safely deposit water into rivers and streams. But sanitary sewer systems cannot do this. The waste they carry must be treated before it can be safely released.

Hundreds of communities in the United States have combined sewer systems. These systems are designed to carry both wastewater and storm water. The two kinds of water are mixed in sewer pipes. After a very heavy rain or snow, the amount of storm water can be too much for the sewer system to handle. The system may overflow, polluting nearby houses, land, and waterways. This is a major health hazard. Sewer workers reduce the threat by helping to design, install, and manage new systems that keep storm water and sewage separate.

After a heavy storm, a sewer system may overflow. This picture shows New Orleans soon after Hurricane Katrina in 2005.

The Main Idea

In cities and towns that have sanitary sewer systems, pipes connect toilets in each home and building to **sewer mains**. Sewer mains are typically made of concrete and are built beneath streets and roads. Smaller mains are connected with each other and with larger mains. The mains get larger and larger as the wastewater flows toward a sewage treatment plant.

Gravity and water pressure are usually enough to move the wastewater through the pipes. In a hilly area, however, pumps or lifts may be needed. (A lift is like an elevator for wastewater.) Pumps and lifts are powered by electricity.

A Subway for Waste

A sewer system in a large city is very complicated. In southern California, for example, the San Diego sewer system serves 1.2 million people. More than 250,000

A Short History of Sewers

Sewers have been around for thousands of years. About 6,000 years ago, people in Babylon (in what is now Iraq) made pipes out of sun-baked clay. More than 4,000 years ago, the people of Mohenjo-Daro (now in Pakistan) had brick-lined streets and sewers. Ancient Rome built a complex water and sewer system more than 2,000 years ago. Wastes and bath water flowed in sewers beneath Rome, emptying into the Tiber River. Modern sanitary sewers and wastewater treatment systems were developed in Europe and the United States in the mid- and late 1800s.

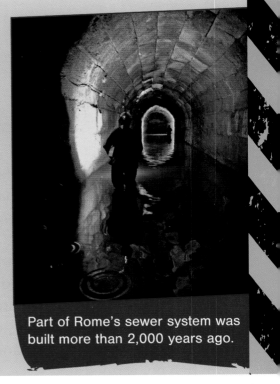

Part of Rome's sewer system was built more than 2,000 years ago.

9

Sewer inspectors must be careful to avoid rats, which can carry diseases.

homes and businesses are linked to sewer lines. The system also includes about 55,000 **manholes**. Manholes allow inspectors and repair crews to enter the system from street level.

In some ways, a large sewer system is like a subway. Both systems run underground. Both provide important city services. Both must be carefully inspected and maintained. Although one system carries people and the other carries waste, failures and accidents in either system can be very serious.

More than Sewage

This treatment plant is run by the Northeast Ohio Regional Sewer District, one of the largest in the United States.

The Northeast Ohio Regional Sewer District runs one of the largest sewer systems in the United States. It covers all or part of more than 60 communities, including the city of Cleveland. The system employs about 600 people. One of them is field tech operator Joe Bitonti. Bitonti started as a sewer inspector when he was 22 years old. He has been inspecting and fixing sewers for more than 30 years.

Taking Off the Cover

One of Joe Bitonti's jobs is to inspect manhole covers to make sure they are not damaged or missing. A manhole cover can weigh up to 200 pounds (90 kilograms) or more. Many covers are made of iron or steel.

Sometimes thieves take the covers and sell them to scrap metal dealers. This leaves an open manhole, which is a danger to people and cars. More than 500 covers were stolen in Philadelphia in 2008. At least two children were injured when they fell into uncovered manholes. In Beijing,

When a manhole cover is stolen, a dangerous open hole is left in the street.

China, thousands of covers are stolen every year. To deal with the problem, judges in China give severe punishments to manhole cover thieves.

After checking the cover, Bitonti's crew must inspect the manhole barrel for cracks and leaks. The barrel is a wide concrete pipe that extends downward from street level to the sewer system below. A metal ladder is attached to the inside of the barrel. Workers use the ladder when they need to enter or leave the sewer system.

Home Treatment

If you live on a farm or in a house in the country, your waste probably does not travel through a sewer system. Instead, a pipe carries the wastewater downward from the toilet and out into the yard. The pipe then empties the wastewater into an underground **septic tank**.

Inside the septic tank, the waste decays, or breaks down. As new wastewater arrives, older water and decayed wastes are forced out of the tank and into a drain field. The drain field is made up of a series of underground pipes surrounded by gravel. These pipes have small holes. The water and decayed wastes seep out of the pipes, through the gravel, and into the ground. The ground then absorbs the water, as the decayed wastes enrich the soil.

Sewer Surprises

Inspectors never know what they will find when they reach the bottom of the manhole barrel. Most sewer inspectors have found some very strange objects. Bitonti remembers finding the bottom part of someone's garage door in a sewer. In the same place, he recalls, inspectors found a 20-foot (6-meter) section of a wooden ladder, along with "four car tires and a Christmas tree complete with decoration! Obviously, someone thought the sewer was their personal Dumpster!"

Sewer inspector Cyndi Sledd works for the Western Virginia Water Authority. She began working as a sewer inspector when she was still a teenager. "The most surprising thing I have found while inspecting a sewer was toys," she says. "Small children's toys that a child had flushed down the toilet." She was amazed that a "whole lot" of toys had traveled through the toilet, clogging the pipe that connected the house to the sewer main.

13

A New York City worker shows some of the waste removed by a treatment plant.

Alive or Dead

More than toys, trees, and sewage are found in sewer systems. In New York City, sewer inspectors have seen just about everything. Each day, New Yorkers discharge at least 1 billion gallons (3.8 billion liters) of wastewater. The city has 14 wastewater treatment plants and more than 6,000 miles (more than 9,650 kilometers) of sewer pipes. The Bureau of Wastewater Treatment, which operates the city's sewer system, has about 1,900 employees and an annual budget of more than $260 million.

Living Underground

Sewers sometimes provide a hiding place for people who cannot stay above ground. During **World War II**, for example, some people in cities in Eastern Europe escaped from the Germans by fleeing underground to the sewers.

Even today, some homeless people hide out in sewers. In April 2009, more than 100 people were found living in sewers beneath train stations in Rome, Italy. Among the homeless were 24 children. Italian police said the children had opened manhole covers at night and slept in the sewer pipes standing up.

Caution: Exploding Manhole Covers!

Sewer gas can be a fire danger. **Methane**, which is contained in sewer gas, can blow up when struck by a spark. If methane builds up below a manhole cover, the explosion can be powerful enough to throw the cover up to 50 feet (15 meters) in the air. One way to guard against methane gas buildup is for inspectors to check for gas leaks. A second way is to use manholes that have small slots. These slots allow the gas to escape a little at a time, before it can cause an explosion.

Sewer inspectors check for gas leaks to help prevent fires like this one in Boston in 2008.

Alligators in the Sewers?

Some people believe that large numbers of alligators live in the sewer system beneath New York City. How do the alligators get there? According to the story, travelers bring in baby alligators from Florida to raise as pets. When the alligators start to grow, their owners flush them down the toilet!

Is this story true? Experts say no. Although New York City inspectors sometimes joke about looking for alligators, no sewer crew working today has ever found one.

There are rumors about alligators living in New York City sewers, but no crew has ever found one.

Sewer workers in New York City have found mattresses, dogs, turtles, fish—even dead people. Bodies of homeless people have been found. "When we get a dead body, we shut down the operation and call the cops," a wastewater treatment supervisor told a reporter for the *New York Times*.

Tree roots can push through the walls of sewer pipes.

Many things can interfere with the flow of wastewater in a sewer. Tree roots can push through the walls of sewer pipes and cause a blockage. Fats, oils, and grease can harden and clog sewer lines. Household objects—either flushed down the toilet or dumped in a manhole—can also cause clogs. Sewer pipes can settle and crack as they age. Over time, these cracks can cause pipes to leak and break. Inspectors must keep a close watch for all these problems.

In a well-run system, inspectors are sent out to check manholes and sewer mains on a regular schedule. That

17

Watch Out for FOG!

Fats, oils, and grease are known by the initials FOG. They can cause major clogs in sewer systems. They can harden into a sticky, gooey mass. Avoid discarding FOG in toilets, sinks, or garbage disposals. Instead, pour the FOG into empty metal cans. Then let the FOG harden and put the can in the trash.

way, small problems can be caught and fixed before they become big ones.

When Sewers Overflow

Storm sewers as well as sanitary sewers must be properly maintained. Even when the systems run in separate pipes, these pipes are often laid side by side. Water that overflows from a blocked storm pipe can force its way into a nearby sanitary sewer. This may cause the sewage to overflow, too.

Overflows can force sewage to back up into toilets and basements. This is dangerous and disgusting. In June 2009, for example, some people living in Elgin, Illinois, had their homes flooded by **raw sewage** after a rainstorm. "Sewage came out of a pipe and shot all over," said one Elgin

Taking Safety Seriously

Experienced sewer inspectors and repair crews use proper equipment. "You should wear your hard hat, steel-toed shoes . . . safety vest and rubber gloves," says Cyndi Sledd, who works in southwestern Virginia. Warning signs and flags are also needed to direct street traffic near the work site.

"The most dangerous work problem I have had to deal with as a sewer inspector is traffic control," Sledd says. "Sometimes cars go by you so fast you don't even see what color they [are]."

Sewer inspectors wear hard hats and rubber gloves to protect themselves.

resident. "Like a volcano!" said another resident. The city planned to spend $160 million to rebuild its sewer system to prevent overflows from storms.

Answering the Call

Sewer inspectors must always be ready to respond to emergencies. People often call to complain about sewage smells and backups. If the problem is in the line connecting a home with the city sewer system, the owner of the home needs to hire someone to repair it. If the problem is in the city's own manholes, storm drains, or sewer mains, the city must handle the repairs.

Many cities have installed devices to monitor, or watch, the flow of water through sewer mains. These devices send information back to a control center. A surge in water flow may indicate a large leak or flood, while a steep drop in water flow may be a sign of a clog. In either case, a sewer inspector will be sent to investigate.

Down in the Hole

About 1.5 million people in the Seattle area are served by the Wastewater Treatment Division of King County, Washington. Pipes in the system range from 12 inches (305 millimeters) to 14 feet (4.3 meters) across. Michael Sands, who works in King County, installs **sensors** that collect data on water flow. He also inspects manholes to make sure they are in good condition.

"Working in a live sewer poses many threats," Sands warns. Workers must use proper safety equipment. When King County workers enter a sewer, they wear protective clothing. Equipment includes coveralls made of Tyvek,

Getting Your Feet Wet

Wastewater treatment plants in several major U.S. cities—including San Francisco, California, and Washington, D.C.—offer public tours. Some tours are regularly scheduled; others may be arranged on request. Some U.S. sewer districts provide summer jobs for high school and college students.

Sewer tours have become a popular option among European travelers. Tourists can visit sewer systems in Paris, France; Brighton, England; Brussels, Belgium; and Vienna, Austria. The classic film *The Third Man* (1950) features a thrilling chase through Vienna's sewers.

Sewer tours are a popular tourist attraction in Vienna, Austria.

How a Wastewater Treatment Plant Works

At a sewage treatment plant, the wastewater to be cleaned must pass through several different stages.

1. As the wastewater enters the plant, it passes through screens. These filter out rocks, pieces of wood, dead animals, and other large items.
2. The wastewater flows (or is pumped) into large tanks or ponds. Scum (including soap and grease) rises to the top and is skimmed off. Solid waste, called sludge, settles to the bottom and is pumped out of the tanks. Scum and sludge are treated in various ways.
3. The remaining water is filtered through sand or other materials to help clean it. A small amount of chlorine is usually added to kill germs.
4. The treatment plant discharges the clean, pure water into a nearby river, stream, or ocean.

a lightweight fabric that keeps sewer waste from getting on workers' skin. Inspectors also wear high rubber boots called **hip waders**, and rubber gloves, which protect against wastewater. Workers may also need to wear a safety harness. The harness has safety straps that prevent falls when a worker goes up or down the ladder connecting the sewer system with the street.

The worst underground hazard, Sands says, is "exposure to hydrogen sulfide gas and low oxygen." If the pipe is full of other gases, workers may not get the oxygen they need. Breathing the wrong gases can make inspectors seriously ill. In extreme cases, the worker can be killed. King County work crews carry an air monitor to make sure the air in a sewer is safe to breathe. If the air is unsafe, workers may need to wear oxygen masks.

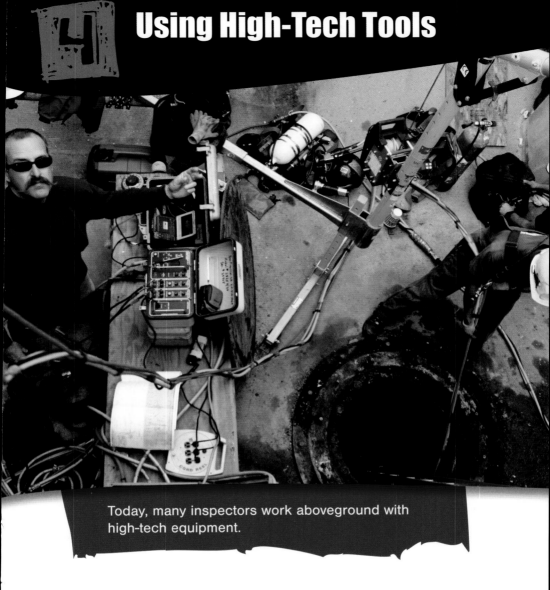

Today, many inspectors work aboveground with high-tech equipment.

One of the least pleasant parts of inspecting a sewer is wading through the muck that flows through it. Today, many inspectors have high-tech tools that help them keep a close watch on sewer flow without getting their hip waders dirty.

New tools allow inspectors to use **lasers** and **sonar** to check for cracks and clogs. Lasers use light beams to

Who Do Sewer Inspectors Work For?

Some sewer systems in the United States are run by private companies. Others are run by cities, counties, or other government units. Inspectors who work for government agencies are known as public employees. Some of these employees belong to a labor union—the American Federation of State, County and Municipal Employees, or AFSCME.

give a highly accurate picture of the interior surface of a pipe. Sonar checks pipes by passing sound waves through sewage. Sonar is the same system that submarines use to find their way underwater.

Testing, Testing . . .

Two methods used by inspectors are smoke testing and dye testing. The smoke used to test sewers is specially made. It can be seen and smelled, but it is designed not to harm people, pets, or plants. Inspectors start by placing a powerful blower over a manhole. The blower forces the smoke down the manhole into the sewer main. If there is a crack or break in the system, the smoke will force its way upward and come out through the ground. Any break where smoke escapes gets close-up inspection, and the break is repaired.

Dye testing can show where storm water is entering a sanitary sewer system. Safe dyes are used to color water, which is then poured down storm drains. Inspectors open nearby manholes to see whether the colored water has mixed with sewage. After trouble spots are found, storm drains and sanitary sewers can be repaired, so that the storm water and sewage are kept separate.

Sewer TV

In 2002, the city of Atlanta, Georgia, launched a $4 billion plan to improve its sewer system. The plan is called Clean Water Atlanta. The city wants to improve water quality, reduce flooding and pollution caused by storm water, and eliminate sanitary sewer spills. All of Atlanta's 60,000 manholes and 2,200 miles (3,540 kilometers) of sewer mains will be inspected for cracks, breaks, and blockages.

Inspectors use computers and TVs to help monitor sewer systems.

SPENT COOKING OIL ONLY

WARNING

This container and its contents are private property pursuant to a contract with the restaurant owner and protected by civil and criminal laws. Tampering or unauthorized removal of contents by any means is strictly prohibited. Removal of any quantity of this container's contents by anyone other than Griffin Industries constitutes theft and will be vigorously prosecuted to the fullest extent of the law.

(800) 782-7147

GRIFFIN
INDUSTRIES

GRIFFIN INDUSTRIES
904-964-8083
INEDIBLE
RECYCLERS SINCE 1943

GRIFFIN INDUSTRIES
904-964-8083
INEDIBLE
RECYCLERS SINCE 1943

This photo shows a recycling bin meant for cooking oil, which is one of the products that should never be flushed down a toilet.

How You Can Help Right Now

You can help sewer systems run smoothly by being careful with toilets and sewers. Never throw anything down a manhole or a sewer grating. Here are some things no one should ever flush down a toilet:

- Stuffed animals (or live ones!)
- Disposable diapers
- Pills and other unused medicines
- Dangerous chemicals or other poisons
- Fats, oils, and grease (FOG)

Inspectors in Atlanta use smoke testing and dye testing. They also use **closed-circuit TV (CCTV)** cameras to carry out many of the inspections. Each camera is mounted on a robot device that can be lowered into a manhole. Inspectors sitting in a truck parked near the manhole view the video signal on a high-resolution TV screen. They can

Serving the Nation's Capital

The Water and Sewer Authority of Washington, D.C., is known as DC WASA. This agency has a very important job. It runs the sewer and water systems for the people who keep the United States government running. DC WASA serves more than 500,000 homes, offices, and businesses in the nation's capital and another 1.6 million users in Maryland and Virginia. Like many other sewer systems, DC WASA uses high-tech inspection methods. Inspectors rely on closed-circuit TV and a combination of CCTV and sonar.

DC WASA operates the Blue Plains Advanced Wastewater Treatment Plant. This plant—one of the largest in the world—can treat up to 1 billion gallons (3.8 billion liters) of wastewater a day.

So You Want to Be a Sewer Inspector

Is sewer inspector the right job for you? Consider these key questions:

Can you work long hours in tight spaces? Sewers are cramped, dirty, and smelly. Inspecting sewers is not pleasant—but it is important.

Can you handle details? You'll need to spot small cracks and leaks before they become big problems. To find your way around a complex sewer system, you'll need to be good at reading maps and plans. You'll also need to write clearly, so repair crews will understand what has to be done.

Are you safety conscious? Sewers can be dangerous places. You'll need to use the right safety equipment the right way. Carelessness causes accidents.

Do you plan to finish high school? Starting jobs require a high school degree or an equivalency diploma. You'll get most of your training on the job.

Do you want steady work at solid pay? There is a constant demand for young inspectors as older ones retire or change jobs. Workers can earn good salaries.

Sewer inspectors must be able to work in small spaces.

steer the robot and TV camera to get a good view of the sewer main. This video is recorded.

Next Steps

After inspectors finish viewing a section of pipe, they grade it on a scale of 1 (best) to 5 (near collapse). If the section needs repair or replacement, the inspectors fill out a work order. The work order describes each specific problem and the exact point on the video recording where the problem can be seen.

Later, a work crew heads down the manhole to do the repair. CCTV robots in Atlanta and other cities let the inspectors stay dry, while the repair crew does the dirty and smelly but important work below ground!

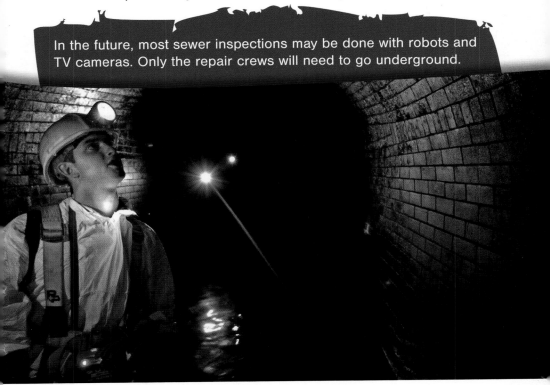

In the future, most sewer inspections may be done with robots and TV cameras. Only the repair crews will need to go underground.

closed-circuit TV (CCTV): A video system that allows staff in a control center to view events in remote locations.

decay: To break down or rot.

gravity: The force that causes things near the surface of Earth to fall.

hip waders: Rubber boots that go as high as the hips.

hydrogen sulfide: A poisonous gas that smells like rotten eggs. This gas, which is found in sewers, is formed when waste matter decays.

laser: A highly focused beam of light that can be used for measuring, cutting, and many other applications.

manhole: A covered place at street level from which inspection and repair crews can enter a sewer system.

methane: An explosive gas formed in sewers when waste matter decays.

raw sewage: Sewer waste that has not been treated in any way.

sanitary sewers: Sewer systems designed to carry wastewater to a sewage treatment plant.

sensors: Devices that collect and transmit data.

septic tank: An underground tank, made of concrete or metal, used in home wastewater treatment systems.

sewage treatment plant: A place where pollutants are removed from wastewater and the water is made clean and pure enough to drink.

sewer mains: Large pipes that carry wastewater to sewage treatment plants.

sonar: A method of using sound waves to detect and locate objects under water.

storm sewers: Sewer systems designed to carry water from rain and melted snow.

wastewater: Water that includes waste products of various kinds.

World War II: A war fought throughout much of the world from 1939 to 1945, in which the Allies (including the United States, the Soviet Union, Britain, and France) defeated the Axis powers (Germany, Italy, and Japan).

BOOKS

Barnhill, Kelly Regan. *Sewers and the Rats That Love Them: The Disgusting Story Behind Where It All Goes*. Mankato, MN: Capstone Press, 2009.

Cooper, Sharon Katz. *Sewers and Gutters*. Chicago: Raintree, 2009.

Frew, Katherine. *Plumber*. New York: Children's Press, 2004.

Miller, Connie Colwell. *Garbage, Waste, Dumps, and You: The Disgusting Story Behind What We Leave Behind*. Mankato, MN: Capstone Press, 2009.

WEBSITES

http://home.howstuffworks.com/homeimprovement/plumbing/sewer.htm
Clear diagrams and explanations show how wastewater is turned into clean water.

http://www.sandiego.gov/mwwd/kids/index.shtml
This "Sewage in Your Face" site, maintained by the City of San Diego, offers facts, games, videos—even recipes for food that "looks like sewage!"

http://www.wef.org/AboutWater/ForStudents/WastewaterTimeline
Enter the "Aquaventurer Time Machine" and explore 10,000 years of water treatment history.

About the Author Geoffrey M. Horn has written more than four dozen books for young people and adults, along with hundreds of articles for encyclopedias and other works. He lives in southwestern Virginia, in the foothills of the Blue Ridge Mountains, with his wife and five cats. His books in the *Dirty and Dangerous Jobs* series are his first for Marshall Cavendish Benchmark. He dedicates this book to the sewer workers who provided generous assistance in describing the work they do in Roanoke, Virginia; Cleveland, Ohio; and Seattle, Washington.